Ulrich Emil Duprée

Ho'oponopono –
The Hawaiian forgiveness ritual as the key
to your life's fulfilment

D1650222

The Book

Ho'oponopono is the Hawaiian ritual of forgiveness. It proceeds from an understanding of the unity of everything in the world, which is true even though we feel ourselves to be separate. Because of this unity or oneness, nothing can happen in our own world without creating a resonance in the observer. It follows that we can only influence problems in the external world if we heal the corresponding inner resonance. To accomplish this, Ho'oponopono relies on four magic sentences: 'I am sorry. Please forgive me. I love you. Thank you.' In this little book Ulrich Emil Duprée describes Ho'oponopono in a simple way that everyone can immediately transform into their own experience.

The Author

Ulrich Emil Duprée, born 1962, is a spiritual seeker and teacher, author and seminar leader. He has studied Christian and Far Eastern philosophies and has lived, among other places, in a Hindu monastery. If you ask him about his profession, he will perhaps answer that he is a builder of bridges who has had a concrete encounter with an angel. Further information available at www.hooponoponosecret.com

Ho'oponopono

The Hawaiian forgiveness ritual
as the key to your life's fulfillment

Ulrich E. Duprée

EARTHDANCER

AN INNER TRADITIONS IMPRINT

Second edition 2014, reprinted 2015, 2016, 2017, 2018, 2019, 2020
First edition published in 2012 by Earthdancer GmbH,
reprinted: 2013

Ulrich Emil Duprée
*Ho'oponopono – The Hawaiian forgiveness ritual as the key
to your life's fulfilment*

Originally published as
Ho'oponopono – Das hawaiianische Vergebungsritual
World Copyright © 2011 Schirner Verlag, Darmstadt

Cover Design: Murat Karaçay, Schirner
Photography: Marina Krasnovid/fotolia.com
and TAlex/fotolia.com

Typesetting: DesignIsIdentity.com
Typeset in Palatino
Printed and bound in China
   by Reliance Printing.

ISBN 978-1-84409-597-1 (print)
ISBN 978-1-84409-894-1 (e-Book)

Published by Earthdancer, an imprint of Inner Traditions
www.earthdancerbooks.com • www.innertraditions.com

MIX
Paper from
responsible sources
FSC® C102842

Contents

Foreword

Dear Reader:

This book is about forgiveness. What is more appropriate than to begin with a dramatic story of sacrifice? It was shortly before Christmas 1970 and I was eight years old when my father bled to death on the carpet in front of me. Why? Was it fair? Did it have any meaning? In my search for answers to these questions, I got to know my first spiritual teacher, the theologian and psychoanalyst Doctor and Professor Joachim Scharfenberg. I have to thank him and his wife, amongst others, for my first glimpses into the world of the Pythagoreans and that of Rudolf Steiner. Since then I have lived as an independent, a traveller, quiet researcher, seminar leader – and also a monk.

In my life I have had the good fortune to be able to walk with great souls and thereby gain an intensive knowledge of two spiritual paths: Christian teachings through my family's side and Hinduism through my studies. These two paths appear outwardly so different, and yet they are the scenery of the same theatre, which in all times and cultures reveals a single truth.

In the course of my search for answers and for the Source of all Being, I have found a key in the Hawaiian forgiveness ritual of Ho'oponopono, and for this I am deeply grateful. At this point I should like to express my thanks and deepest respect for all those who, all across the world, have left various keys behind them, and will do so in the future too.

Protected by the remoteness of a small group of islands in the middle of the Ocean of Peace, a simple but very effective method has survived the centuries. I should like to acquaint you with this blossom from Hawaii, which is quite tender and fragile, even holy, and so exists as the most effective method of solving conflicts and problems. Welcome to the world of the Ho'oponopono.

The Story of Ho'oponopono

The roots of Ho'oponopono reach far back into the past. Some say even to the time of Atlantis, Lemuria and the High Vedic Culture. Ho'oponopono belongs to a system of ancient Hawaiian teaching called the 'Huna'. 'Hu' means 'knowledge', and 'na' represents 'wisdom', and the guardians of this ancient teaching are called 'kahunas' – Huna experts. Only to know something without then using it really makes nonsense of it, because wisdom is revealed by what a person does, not by what they know. Ho'oponopono also comes alive when it is used, and so I invite you into this little book and thereby to walk in a world full of wisdom, wonder and beauty; a world whose existence you have always suspected, but could never grasp until now.

The Hawaiians call their group of islands 'The Land of Aloha', The Land of Love. 'Aloha' contains the essence of the Huna teaching of knowledge and wisdom, and it forms the basis of Ho'oponopono. 'Aloha' means, 'I see the divine in you, and I see the divine in myself.' This carries the understanding that you and I, your neighbour and the President in the White House, all of us travel a common road, and that there is only one power in the Universe, namely the energy of unconditional love, 'mana aloha' in Hawaiian. Aloha has only a single commandment: never to harm, always to help. The command to harm no one begins with not harming oneself. And thus, to love your neighbour as yourself. 'Mana aloha' is the essence of God's energy, the energy that penetrates and informs everything. The wise Hindu monks with whom I was allowed to live called this energy 'bhakti', meaning 'devotion', and the Tibetan monks whom I also encountered called it 'compassion'. By this, they did not merely have in mind an emotion, but a directly experienced energy that influences the environment and creates a new reality. Ho'oponopono is this compassion in action, and therefore it is the theme of this book.

According to a story from humankind's begin-nings, the problems of the world arose when we fell into the error of thinking that instead of only one power, there were two: good and evil. Instead of compassion and its logical consequence, the realisation that all is one, judgment and condemnation entered human thinking. Humankind took a step away from unity into separation – the first so-called advance in our history.

Ho'oponopono is a simple way of arriving at unity, inner peace and returning to harmony. Ho'oponopono implies solving a problem from the ground up and applying the solution to useful ends. It expresses the deep need to live once again in harmony with oneself and with humanity, nature and God. *Ho'o* means 'to make' and *pono* is translated 'right' or 'correct'. It follows that *ponopono* would be 'rightly right' and so *ho'oponopono* quite simply represents 'to make rightly right'. To 'make anything rightly right' means to join oneself again with one's Higher Self and the Source of All Being – to be in one's own centre, returned to harmony, and balanced once again so that one is able to realign the environment and reshape reality. To 'make rightly right' means an undertaking, after veering off course, to bring oneself back onto the right road, becoming sound in body and spirit and achieving happiness and wellbeing.

Ho'oponopono means a return to the divine plan, and is also described as a path to perfection.

What is Ho'oponopono?

The Paradigm Change

Ho'oponopono is a spiritual-soul method of purification that cleanses us from fears and worries, destructive relationship patterns, and any religious dogmas and paradigms that oppose our personal and spiritual development. It cleans out the blockages in our thoughts and cell structure, for our thoughts are made manifest in our body. This is the paradigm change.

This method is of Hawaiian origin and is based on the understanding that we live in a Universe of abundance and that God ('Akua', the original Source) wants us to enjoy this abundance and perfection. However, what obstructs our experience of real abundance, loving togetherness, inner wealth, spiritual growth and perfect health is our own self. It is our thinking, grounded and reinforced by a great deal of experience, which for a long time now has lost its validity. Its persistent attachment to fears and cares, to judgments, doubt and the negative mass consciousness frustrates our experience of our own perfection.

Imagine that you are holding a big stone in each hand. If I should want to give you some money right now, you must first put the stones aside. The same applies to our patterns and prejudices, our values and the gifts of the Universe. The key to being able to receive, lies in the ability to let something go, in the faith that we will not suffer any harm or loss thereby.

The forgiveness ritual of Ho'oponopono is love in action. You forgive yourself and others for having inflicted any sort of hurt, or for having failed to help when needed. 'Making things rightly right' is a simple four-step procedure that helps you learn to forgive yourself unconditionally, to love, and, additionally, to make things better. It is as if you were reformatting your computer's hard disk. It wipes out all the data that makes your life slow and burdensome.

If something disturbs us and we feel disharmony within ourselves, maybe recognise a problem or a conflict, we can always make a simplified Ho'oponopono.

1. We ask to reach a place of recognition, courage, power, intelligence and peace.

2. We describe the problem and then search our heart for our share in it. This share may, for example, be a judgment we have made, or a specific action, or a memory that requires healing.

3. We forgive unconditionally and speak the four magic sentences: I am sorry. Please forgive me. I love you. Thank you.

4. We give thanks, express trust and let go.

This simple and elegant method will not only ensure the resolution of personal problems and challenges, but also resolve conflicts within a community or group. Thus a Ho'oponopono will demonstrate its effectiveness in all the realms of partnership and family, profession, health and finance. In his book *Zero Limits*,* which he has written with Dr. Ihaleakala Hew Len, Dr. Joe Vitale plainly hallows this system in the subtitle: *The Secret Hawaiian System for Wealth, Health, Peace and More*.

We know today that in Hawaii the forgiveness ritual forms the preparation for the healing of a physical

* Vitale Joe/Hew Len, Ihaleakala: *Zero Limits. The Secret Hawaiian System for Wealth, Health, Peace and More*. Wiley 2007.

illness. Sicknesses are seen as symptoms of inner conflict, and the energetic tensions are released through a shamanistic Ho'oponopono ritual. When the soul is healed, the body follows.

From the publications of the Hawaiian Eldest Mary Kawena Pukui (1895 - 1986) in the 1950s, we know Ho'oponopono as a traditional family conference. Misunderstandings and misdemeanours are here reviewed and discussed in the presence of a mediator *(haku).* In the problem-solving process *(kalana)* all the participants look into their hearts before God and those present, and all aspects of anger, disappointment, resistance and mistrust are resolved in unconditional forgiveness. In the 1970s, Hawaii's living treasure, the revered Morrnah Nalamaku Simeonah (1913 - 1992), introduced a modernised twelve-step method to the public. She integrated Christian and Indian elements as well as the system of the three selves (subconscious, conscious, superconscious) and presented Ho'oponopono as an aid to self-help. It thereby became possible to apply this technique to the purification of mind and soul without a mediator.

After Morrnah Nalamaku Simeonah's death in 1996, her pupil Dr. Ihaleakala Hew Len took over the leadership of her institute, 'Foundation of I'. It was through him and his healing of psychologically ill prisoners that Ho'oponopono became known in the West. Dr. Len teaches Ho'oponopono among other things as the purification of memories, meaning the purifying of any data that inhibits harmony. Inward forgiveness and the method of love can in this sense be understood as a simplified Ho'oponopono.

We can see that Ho'oponopono is not a rigid system, but that a common thread runs through all its variations. In this little book you will learn two of them in summary and for immediate aid: first, Ho'oponopono as a method of purification through which you can rid yourself of inner blockages and programs that sabotage the free flow of life (e. g., I have doubts) and the gifts of the Universe (e. g., I have not deserved this); and second, Ho'oponopono in the form of family conference – as it is traditionally practiced in Hawaii and applied in youth and social work.

To be successful, it is important to take the following steps:

1. To join with the Original Source (Akua), the Being of Light and the Ancestors.
2. To contemplate and accept the problem (Hala, Hihia).
3. To take on 100% responsibility for the existence of the problem in your life.
4. To be ready, following forgiveness, to handle things differently.
5. To mutually pardon and forgive (Mihi)
6. To give thanks and offer the closing prayer (Pule Ho'opau).

All situations, encounters and events that enter my experiential horizon have meaning, and through Ho'oponopono you can learn to decipher these inward, hidden messages that are contained in the situations and events.

Ho'oponopono is practice-oriented and while you read this little book, you can already start undoing the Gordian knot in your heart and get ready to shape your world afresh.

The Story of Dr. Ihaleakala Hew Len

Ho'oponopono may be the most effective method of solving problems and conflicts ever devised by a culture. It became known mainly through Dr. Ihaleakala Hew Len and the record of his work in healing some psychologically ill prisoners. This achievement is considered a therapeutic miracle, and demonstrates the effectiveness of Ho'oponopono. Moreover, it is an acknowledged therapy in the USA, and even for forgiveness at the diplomatic level there are already more than 50 studies.

In 1983 a trusted friend asked Dr. Ihaleakala Hew Len to work in the psychiatric department of the state prison of Kaneohe on Hawaii. Thirty prisoners, all psychologically ill, were confined there, with a chronic shortage of staff. There was good reason for this shortage because both the institution and the work were commonly described as 'the hell'. Most of the employees were either ill, unsuited for the work or gave in their notice as soon as possible after beginning employment. However, Dr. Ihaleakala Hew Len agreed to work there – on condition that he was allowed to use a method that he had just learnt. It was arranged that he would only read the prisoners' reports and would not talk with them.

What did Dr. Ihaleakala Hew Len do? In the following four years he read the prisoners' reports several times daily and asked himself, 'What is there in me of darkness and negativity, of power and hatefulness, that something similar should exist in my world? What is my part in it that my brother has done such a thing?' When he found something of that in himself and in his heart (power, aggression, hatred, vengefulness, envy, jealousy – the whole palette of the depths of humanity), he would say:

I am sorry. Please forgive me.
I love you. Thank you.

Dr. Ihaleakala Hew Len worked exclusively on the cleansing of his heart and consciousness and after one and a half years he had made a Ho'oponopono and changed the mood, atmosphere and climate in the prison hospital. After 18 months, none of the prisoners wore handcuffs anymore. The staff, wardens and therapists now came happily to work and the illness figures declined. It became possible to hold therapeutic conversations with the prisoners, and after four years all the inmates, except for two, were cured. The institution was finally closed.

Did Dr. Ihaleakalal Hew Len really cure anyone? Those impacted say, 'Yes'. However, in an interview Dr. Ihaleakala Hew Len has explained that he only worked on his own purification and the deleting of information in his own subconscious. He did not speak of cures, but emphasized that the solution to the respective conflicts succeeded because he had taken 100% responsibility for the existence of the prisoners in his life.

The Power of Forgiveness

Destructive thoughts about past events improve neither the world nor our life in it. Quite the opposite: the smouldering fires of old disappointments, of annoyance and rage, or a toxic mental cocktail composed of jealousy and resentment only make the heart heavier and gloomier. We tend to turn away from people who have the smell of sarcasm about them.

Once upon a time there were two monks who in the course of their wanderings came to a river. Sitting there was a young woman who said, 'I cannot swim. If you, O worthy sages, also want to cross this river, I would be very grateful if one of you would carry me over.' One of them said at once, 'Come and climb on my shoulders,' and together all three crossed the river. On the other side of the river the woman bade them goodbye and the monks travelled on. They did not talk, but one of them seemed troubled by something. 'What is it, my friend? You look annoyed,' said the one who had carried the woman. At that, the other snapped, 'Oh, you fool, how could you have any contact with a woman? We are monks and live withdrawn from the world.' To which the other replied, 'It's true, I have carried that woman across the river. But from what I hear, it seems to me that you are still carrying her.'

Forgiveness releases us. It frees us from a burden that either we cannot carry or do not want to carry. Who would want to live their life with a big backpack on their shoulders, full of problems, old conflicts and fears? Forgiveness heals and makes life easier. Above all, forgiveness is a gift that we give to ourselves. In Hawaii, after the forgiving, the matter is settled and no one busies themselves with it any longer.

Forgiveness is not a one-time thing
Forgiveness is a life-style

Dr. Martin Luther King

We can learn forgiving and forgetting – just like every-thing else, just like running or painting. If it does not work out straight away, we can act as if it did. It works like an affirmation, e. g. 'I am pretty and my body is well formed' – it sounds completely absurd, but say it enough times and you might come to say, 'Yes, yes, it's true, I can see it.' Interestingly, other people will then see it too, and we are proven right. To a considerable degree, we experience what we send out into the world with our thoughts and feelings. The world seems to resemble a great mirror, for it reflects whatever it is we feel deep in our hearts.

In Ho'oponopono we call it the *kuolo* – the resonance of the outer world upon our inner world. The problems, sickness, strife, poverty, environmental destruction, famine and wars, are the image of the inner disturbances of humanity. Things have got out of harmony and in Ho'oponopono we seek the way back to peace while we heal the problem in ourselves.

The Core of the Simplified Ho'oponopono: The Four Magic Sentences

Together we will apply the four magic sentences of the Ho'oponopono in small exercises and examples to solve problems and conflicts. It is quite simple, so please take part in this. If something troubles you, if something sends prickles up your spine and you would like best to turn around and go away, and above all, if someone 'presses your buttons', always direct your thoughts to the following sentences:

> I am sorry
> Please forgive me
> I love you
> Thank you

These four sentences seem like a mantra or a magical formula, but they are rather a meditation and a prayer. They operate through time and space, beyond cause and effect, and transmit themselves directly to your Inner Family, the Higher Self (aumakua), the Inner

Child *(unihipili)* and your waking consciousness *(uhane)*. After a short while you achieve inner peace, and change from disharmony to harmony. You move yourself from separation to union while you say:

I am sorry. Please forgive me.
I love you. Thank you.

What do these four sentences mean?

I am sorry
I apologise. I perceive that I suffer, and that connects me to my feelings. I no longer reject the problem, but recognise my learning task. I or my forebears (with whom I am connected energetically, genetically and by tradition as much as by history) have caused harm. I know where I stand and feel remorse.

Please forgive me
Please forgive me for having, through myself or my forebears, consciously or unconsciously disturbed you and me in the course of our evolution. Please forgive

me for having acted contrary to the divine laws of harmony and love. Please forgive me for having until now judged you (or the situation), and in the past disregarded our spiritual identity and connectedness.

I love you

I love you and I love myself. I see and respect the divine in you. I love and accept the situation just as it is. I love the problem that has come to me to open my eyes. I love you and myself unconditionally with all our weaknesses and faults.

Thank you

Thank you, for I understand that the miracle is already underway. I thank God and the angels for the transformation of my request. I give thanks, because what I have received and what will come to pass is what I have deserved through the law of cause and effect. I give thanks because, through the power of forgiveness, I am now freed from the energetic chains of the past. I give thanks that I may recognise and join with the Source of all Being.

When you arise in the morning,
give thanks for the morning light,
for your life and the power that you possess.
If you see no reason
to give thanks, that is your business.

Tecumseh

The word 'problem' originally comes from the Greek and refers to a task or a dispute. Literally translated, it means 'The Gods throw a stone before our feet.' The rulers of Fate and Olympus do not do this to annoy us, but to ensure that we grow because of it. Every problem is a challenge and offers a learning exercise. We may grow through every challenge, whether it is about a new colleague, a neighbour, a traffic jam, an illness, a family crisis or a hole in the savings account. People and problems that we perhaps see as our foes, are really our best friends, because they show us where we have to work. We could also say, life consists of a linked sequence of tests that show us where we stand.

A Ho'oponopono Exercise

Please lean back a little and think of a problem that is occupying you or a good friend. Visualise this problem and search for it within yourself. What feelings come up? Breathe peacefully and be relaxed. Observe your feelings and the problem. Now say the four sentences and read the clarifications relating to each. Remain an observer. Repeat the four magic sentences to yourself until a feeling of understanding and sympathy arises. Give thanks.

We are used to seeing our world in dualistic terms. We see things as simple or hard, above or below, rich or poor, black or white. It is like a coin. There is only one coin, but we see two sides. That is precisely the way we see our personal and international conflicts. We see ourselves and we see the conflict. We see a victim (perhaps ourselves). Then we say, 'The other is guilty,' and by that we mean that the other owes us for spoiling our happiness. It would be interesting if we were to question those we consider culpable: those whom we make responsible for our unease, for having stolen our happiness, those who threaten us, harm us or whom we oppose, those whom we avoid in the workplace or make way for in the street, or those who easily provoke us. If you were to ask these people why they act in this way, you would probably hear one of the following answers: 'I do my best and can really do no different.' 'But this is what you wanted!' 'I am a victim of society and circumstance...' In other words, nearly every culprit describes him or herself as a victim.

Though it will be discussed later in the book, it is interesting to view conflicts in terms of the Ho'opono-pono practice of Family Conference. In social work and couple counselling, the participants in the conflict ask themselves directly how they have contributed to the problem, and they appeal for unconditional forgiveness and grant the same themselves. No one looks for compromise but the greatest possible consensus, and each meets the other on a higher spiritual plane.

However, back to our metaphor. Victim and culprit cancel out. They are like the two sides of a coin. If I no longer reject my illness, my colleague or my debts, but integrate and use them as the springboard for growth and knowledge, I have made a leap towards perfection. I am reclaiming for myself the power to shape my world.

> *Experience is not what happens to you.*
> *Experience is what you make out of what happens to you.*
>
> Aldous Huxley

We seldom have any influence over the actions of others, but we can decide what we think of them, how we feel about them and what consequences to expect. We can choose to make ourselves the prisoners of our own thoughts, or to liberate ourselves and grow.

The often-experienced world view of victims is that the problem is too large and they can do nothing about it. Ho'oponopono turns this on its head because we see that…

… the problem is close to me, and on that account I have something to do about it.

… if I change myself, I can change something.

…   I can change myself and therefore have the power to make other changes.

Please step out of the shadows and take back your power to make changes.

Ho'oponopono works as a powerful tool to solve conflicts. Keep a simple trust in the power of love and forgiveness, and just say:

I am sorry. Please forgive me.
I love you. Thank you.

A Hoʻoponopono Exercise

Lean back a little and think of a person about whom you have some reservations, perhaps you avoid them or even argue with them. Feel deeply within yourself, and now become aware of your strongest, central feeling. Become an observer. Observe and describe this feeling as precisely as possible. Embrace it in a single word (e. g., fear, sadness, anger…). Take a deep breath and say, 'Just like me, this person has experienced … (name the feeling). This person experiences … (name the feeling) just like me, and I feel it with him. I am sorry. Please forgive me. I love you. Thank you.' Please repeat this exercise and carefully read the clarifications of the four sentences one more time. Thank you.

Ho'oponopono and the Spiritual Laws

The Law of Cause and Effect – *ka ua mea*

We live in a Universe of cause and effect. Each thought, each feeling and each word is based on something that happened earlier. Everything we do, and also everything we don't do (e.g., by refusing or ignoring our ability to help), has an energetic effect. This means that every single one of our thoughts, words and deeds, have a respective effect, which on their side works as the cause of new activity and thereby becomes a new effect. Through regression we encounter a gigantic network of causes and effects. This law of causality holds the Universe in energetic balance. On the material plane it brings about the constant transformation of all substances, and on the spiritual plane it guarantees our learning process: we reap what we sow.

The sicknesses of civilisation, environmental catastrophes, increasing violence in our schools – are these chance happenings? No, they are the results of what humankind, individually and as a collective, does and does not do. The law of cause and effect binds human beings to their actions, and as a spiritual law, it makes the consequences foreseeable. There is no punishing God. It is the emotionless principle of causality that directs what happens.

Everything is Connected to Everything Else

The following phenomenon was observed in a quantum physics experiment: the researcher split a photon (a source of light) and sent both twin particles to two positions that were 14 km distant. When the spin of one of the particles was altered, the spin of the other particle was also immediately altered (simultaneously!). This connectivity is called quantum entanglement. The subatomic particles are figuratively interlocked with one another, such that as soon as the behaviour of one particle is altered, the twin quantum alters too. What was once connected, remains connected.

Yet it is also quite understandable that your body is composed in part of atoms and molecules that were perhaps carried by one of my ancestors, or Julius Caesar or Nefertiti. Everything on Earth belongs to the substance of this planet, and thus, just as we are joined together in the material, so on the subtle planes we are joined through our Spirit. Our consciousness is a part of the ever-present and all-penetrating World Soul. Each one of us bears within ourselves an aspect of

God. In addition we have a Higher Self, a collective subconscious and an archetypical conscience. Thus, whether regarded physically, mathematically, chemically, musically or spiritually – we are all, you and I, human and animal, plants and nature, joined with each other. Together we form a whole and at the same time are individuals.

Here I should like to describe to you an astonishing phenomenon that has recently been discovered by newly developed measurement processes and reported by the Institute of HeartMath: the electromagnetic field produced by the heart has a measurable radius of approximately eight metres. This means that we mutually penetrate each other, whether in a cinema, on a bus, in the waiting-room, everywhere, and simultaneously we penetrate each other with our feelings, wishes and plans.

Everything that once was, still is,
only in another form.

Hopi Wisdom

Everything is Vibration

In the beginning was the Word, the Logos, the sound, the syllable OM (Aum) and the original chord. Everything vibrates. In this Universe there is no standing still. Everything oscillates, pulsates rhythmically, circles and moves in cycles. Everything flows, as the ancient Greeks used to say; at every moment several thousand micro-chemical processes take place in each single cell of your body.

Sound makes mood. We often speak of 'good vibrations' or 'a bad atmosphere' (vibes). We have an 'antenna' for that sort of thing and, when we enter a space, we know in our hearts 'where the music plays'. The Universe is a kind of mighty symphony, and it is because everything vibrates and is connected each-to-each that everything also mutually influences everything else. All atoms send out and receive energy. Through the so-called principle of resonance, similar vibrations collect together. Like attracts like.

Just as wave crests reinforce the oscillating ebb and flow, contrasting oscillations are to be found in the culprit-victim relationship. Just as wave crests and valleys succeed and reinforce each other, we also see this mutual strengthening in teamwork or in a committed partnership. In a team, one plus one are worth more than two individuals, because they are mutually inspired, challenged and encouraged. On the other hand, if contrasting oscillations cancel out, we soon recognise whether or not our colleagues are in sync with us. Both parties can still contribute many skills – or achievement lags.

Every conflict, every judgment, condemnation, unhappiness and complaint leads not only to a decline of energy ('I am busy!'), but also to dissonance and discord ('I can no longer listen to that'). This disharmony opposes love and leads to sickness and separation ('I want to get away'). By contrast, harmony and sincere sympathy lead to health and unity. Because everything influences everything else, I contribute to harmony if I discover my share in disharmony and enter instead into the healing process. I am a part of this world. While I heal myself, I heal the world. If there is a disturbance anywhere, I feel it in myself. If in this way I find my share in the disturbance and enter into harmony again, I am participating actively in the world's healing process.

A Ho'oponopono Exercise

Please read over the last section once again and check in what situations you feel the urge to stop listening, and when you want get away. Please write these situations down and recognize that here are some experiences that want healing and resolution.

Make a Ho'oponopono for every situation while accepting these situations as learning tasks. Meditate upon them and repeat the four magic sentences.

I am sorry. Please forgive me.
I love you. Thank you.

Forgive yourself for having brought such situations on yourself in the past. Simply give up all your opposition, for everything against which we defend ourselves only comes back against us with even greater power.

Humankind, Spirit of God's Spirit – *kane*

We are far more than this physical body. We are also far more than our thoughts. We are not this body, but we have this body. We are also not our thoughts, but we have thoughts, and even they are frequently not our own, but rather a reflection on the headlines of a huge daily newspaper, for example.

We, you and I, animals and plants, are spiritual beings. The core of our true identity is divine. It is that which does not age, but always was and ever will be. In Hebrew this immaterial divine spark is called 'odem', and in Sanskrit 'atma'. The Huna concept is expressed 'kane', Spirit of God's Spirit. Just as a drop of water from the ocean possesses all the chemical properties and elements of the ocean, so too in our pure consciousness we have all the qualities of God – though only in small measure. In quality we are like God, but in quantity we are different. Thus, you and I are not material beings who are having a spiritual experience. On the contrary, by our nature we are non-physical, spiritual beings who are having a material experience, and we all find ourselves on a common journey.

Imagine that you are stuck in a traffic jam. If you have no important and pressing goal in mind, you can contemplate the matter in a relaxed fashion. Admittedly, if your work, relationship or even someone's life were at stake, the matter would look quite different. For one person, a traffic jam can be a saving grace, for another a complete catastrophe.

From a Buddhist point of view, every situation, event and object is essentially empty. Everything gains meaning by our contemplating it. Among the Huna this translates as 'the world is what we think it is'. Our world is subjective.

It is clear to us all that the world is far more than we, with our limited senses, can perceive. The ranges and perceptive spectra of our eyes, ears, nose, skin and tongue are limited and individually different. Simultaneously, our brain filters only that which appears important to us and our cultural conditioning from the flood of information and mob of data reaching us. The world works on us, and we sense reality as a result of our past experiences. This past, our thoughts and feelings, our learnt opinions and their interpretations, all form our world. From truth there is formed a reality – one that operates on us.

> *You are today where your thoughts*
> *have brought you, and tomorrow you will be*
> *where your thoughts will bring you.*
>
> James Allen

With every thought and every word we create our future. If we think lovingly and sympathetically, we are the co-creators of a harmonious future. Thoughts full of doubt, aversion and bitterness will relegate us to be the co-creators of a gloomy future. Thoughts and words of love and forgiveness raise the vibrations. Thoughts of worthlessness and condemnation lower the vibrations. It remains up to us to decide which film we enjoy, what we like eating, what we believe and where we work.

The Spirit of Ho'oponopono

Peace Begins With Me

The management expert and psychologist Anthony Robbins reports that success in his seminars on Personality Development and Neurolinguistic Programming (NLP) depends on the individual's experiences, and these experiences are based mainly on mistakes. Past errors, like a company bankruptcy or a wrecked marriage, only become mistakes if we do not learn from them. Otherwise they are merely events and experiences.

For many years I felt annoyed and inwardly belittled myself for my mistakes. I resented those who had harmed me and frequently thought about them, so continuing to allow them mental force and power over me. The healing of my soul began in a literary encounter with Louise Hay. She recommended me to love myself. 'I forgive myself. I am sorry. I love myself. Thank you.'

A Ho'oponopono Exercise

Look into your past to find a mistake or error of judgment for which you cannot forgive yourself. Observe it from a distance. Look closely at the event and appreciate it as something that has contributed to your learning process. (Do not imagine that you could have spared yourself this error. If you had not made it, it would still be approaching you.) Now forgive yourself for having been annoyed about it for so long. Then say the four magic sentences and let go of it forever.

Forgiveness is an effective mental and physical antidote to poison. Negative thoughts poison our body. First the soul becomes sick and then the body.

Constant stress, impatience and ill humour sour the body and poison the cells. Untimely aging, loss of drive and depression are the usual consequences. A guilt-laden spirit becomes melancholy, but if we love and forgive ourselves despite our past faults, we strengthen our immune system and rejuvenate.

It is not possible to alter other people, but everyone can begin with themselves and in this way act as a model for others. This world can experience peace if we find harmony within ourselves, are at rest within and do not look only for external happiness. If we have peace within ourselves, we can pass it on. People change when they themselves want to change direction.

Ho'oponopono Prayer (Pule)

Dear God, Father and Mother, Source of all Being, you are our best friend, thank you, thank you, thank you. We face a great challenge and we ask for your blessing in this Ho'oponopono that all may grow together. We give thanks for the strength to say the truth and for the courage to listen to the truth. We give thanks for your divine guidance. Thank you.

There is only one corner of the universe
you can be certain of improving,
and that's your own self.

Aldous Huxley

Healing the Past

Over a lifetime, events can happen that leave behind wounds that are hard to heal. Perhaps we were wounded in the body or soul. Perhaps we were victims of ill treatment. Whatever it was, we cannot undo what was done, but we *can* remove its harmful influence from our past.

The past lives in us in the form of memories. It is still present in us, and the meanings we attach to events from the near or distant past are directed by our current feelings. Do we accord to others the right to determine how we speak, act or think? No.

When we change the feelings that link us to events, we also change our memory, and when we change our memory, we change our view of the present and the future. Sometimes that necessitates long years of therapy, but with a Ho'oponopono this quantum leap often succeeds within a few minutes.

The Moment of Power is Now

I would like now to invite you to just such a quantum leap. The driving force behind our actions is our subconscious, and we, or rather someone, has programmed our subconscious. Perhaps your parents believed you to be a failure, or you have a partner who tries to control you, while telling you how bad you are. The fact is: the only thing that counts is what you believe. Only what you believe about yourself, your self-image, counts.

A Hoʻoponopono Exercise
Morning and evening, please place yourself before a mirror and repeat ten times intensely:

I am sorry. Please forgive me.
I love you… (your first name). Thank you.

Perhaps the change does not happen straight away, and you even become enraged or saddened.

However it may be, if you have not loved your-self over long years, it is hard to suddenly love yourself from now on. We live by our habits, and perhaps we must first get in the habit of loving ourselves. That is not egotistical but sen-sible. Make a habit of loving yourself. Thinking negatively about yourself and others is only a habit. It is one you can give up.

Examples of liberating sentences:

- I am sorry that I still cannot completely love myself.

- I am sorry that I still cannot completely absolve and forgive.

- I now open myself to love for myself and love for you.

- I love the world, I love humankind, I love nature and I love you, Source of all Being and give you wholehearted thanks for my life.

Two are always necessary to start a conflict, even when we wrangle with ourselves, and the whole question revolves around an inner dialogue of nagging self-doubt. The problem is always mine, because I am part of the problem. I have a share in it, even when I am not the obvious cause. If I accept that there is a vibe in me that is attracted to the disturbance through the principle of resonance, I move from impotence to power and can contribute something to the solution.

We are frequently accustomed to react to circumstances, events and people. For us to take 100% responsibility for everything that comes into our life means that we make the leap from reaction to action. The trainer and entrepreneurial adviser Stephen R. Covey calls this becoming proactive. Taking 100% responsibility means understanding that I dispose of the free decision to choose my reactions. If we understand ourselves as spiritual beings, we recognise the equality of all living beings and can develop the qualities of sympathy, understanding and equanimity in ourselves.

> *The weak cannot forgive*
> *Forgiveness is a quality of the strong.*
>
> Mahatma Gandhi

Reviewing all my past personal conflicts, I can see that my opponents were only seeking understanding, just like myself. Meet whomever with pure sympathy, without offering appreciation or depreciation, and their defences fall. How often have I gone to battle or resisted because I felt myself misunderstood? The secret of the success of the Ho'oponopono problem-solving process lies in its taking a backward step and appreciating nobody and nothing. Through the consequent lack of all judgment, the Universe can proceed in harmony and reveal new, hitherto unsuspected solutions. Try it out.

A Ho'oponopono Exercise

Now look for a problem regarding environmental protection, one in which you feel powerless and forced to believe that there are people involved who are responsible for the destruction of the natural world.

Visualise the problem with all its outcomes, which are so terrible for you. Now ask yourself, what is your share in this conflict? What things do you use that contribute to the problem and justify the behaviour of these people? Now do a Ho'oponopono. Your subconscious has known for a long time that you are not in harmony with your conscious values and are experiencing an inner conflict. Now forgive yourself unconditionally, and forgive yourself and everyone else for their behaviour. Repeat the four magic sentences for a whole day while you observe yourself, and look for constructive ways to do something for the natural world. Give thanks.

There is nothing in this world that is unimportant or of little worth. Everything has its meaning and is an expression of the life within it. Everything is reality. The two syllables 're' and 'al' originate from ancient Egyptian. 'Re' indicates 'God' and 'al' can be understood as 'penetrating, existing'. In priestly language, the word 'real' describes the all-penetrating existence of God, the all-present and complete hologram, which is the absolute truth. In other words: There is only God.

In the story of the so-called Fall, the material Ego – which is the false projection of what I am – tried to split away from God, from reality, and in its fear created a number of relative truths. Since then, people can say, 'Everything is relative.' Lies have been explained as truths, and the law established that Might is Right. In this new, materialist environment those who thought differently and 'uncivilized peoples' were indeed valued like beasts of little worth. They had no rights, must be taught and could be killed. Only while it promulgated the triumph of its expansion could the false understanding of ego compensate for its lack of worth, and dismiss as a 'special case' everything that did not suit its concept. One of these false projections ran as follows: 'If I have more, then I am worth more, and if I do not have it, then I am worth less.'

In the 1990s I was a publisher. I still remember the precise feeling of suddenly being something special. It stayed for about a week and then the everyday feeling was back. The only thing that had changed was my professional designation, but I – I had not changed at all.

Things went worse for a Boston man, as Bill Ferguson reported in his much recommended audio program, *The Mastery of Life*. I have to thank Bill Ferguson and his audio program for many important endorsements. For further information see www.masteryoflife.com. This man slaved and saved to somehow fulfil his dream: a 1-million dollar house. He took it so far as to actually buy a house in an upper-class district and feel himself someone special – for a few hours anyway. For when he made a tour of the neighbourhood, he realised that he had bought the smallest house in the quarter. Utterly floored, shocked and feeling hugely inferior, he made life hell for his wife: Why had she not paid more attention? She left him, and as far as I recollect the story, the house was sold.

At times our relationship with our mistakes takes some bizarre forms, for example when people define themselves by their pain and fall in love with their problems. The brain then builds up a neural network, and we are always finding fresh reasons for feeling bad and therefore why we are just as we are – namely, not good enough. We might think that our parents, our upbringing and circumstances are to blame. At the centre of all this pain is, and is still, the false understanding of our identity, that is, the material ego with its three weapons: fear, separation and guilt.

A Ho'oponopono Exercise

Lean back, ease up and give your thoughts free rein. When do you feel yourself better, more enlightened, more human, more respected than other people? On what occasions is it so good to be a German, a Spaniard, a white man, an Indian, a man or a woman, because the others don't even 'have a clue'? Visualise these situations. Now make a Ho'oponopono and ask for forgiveness from all those whom you have considered of less worth. As a second step, make a Ho'oponopono and ask yourself for all the opportunities for forgiveness in which you felt yourself to be less worthy. Give thanks – you have contributed directly to world peace.

Our senses are imperfect and according to the testimony of the Ayurveda, nine out of ten conclusions are simply wrong. Our objectivity is reduced to 10%. Judgment leads to separation. Acceptance and forgiveness lead back to unity. Separation leads to disharmony, isolation, fear, arrogance and sickness. Harmony and agreement on the other hand lead to joy, happiness, inner riches (and if one so wishes, outer riches follow) and health. God, the Universe and Source do not pass judgment for they know that in every second we do everything possible for ourselves. When we judge, we raise ourselves above God.

Examples of liberating sentences:

- I am sorry that I want to be perfect. I am sorry that I believe that I will only be worth loving if I am perfect. I suffer for it, and so does everything around me.
- Please forgive me. I forgive myself for that now. I ask you to forgive me and I now forgive myself unconditionally. I now forgive everyone who has made me afraid and who now have such a great claim on me and on themselves. I love myself in my imperfection, as I love a child in its imperfection. I now acknowledge my perfection, just as a child is perfect. I now accept myself, just as God accepts me. Thank you, thank you, thank you.

Spiritual Intelligence

The aim of Ho'oponopono and the Aloha principle is to stop making judgments, and to strengthen the capacity for discrimination. Spiritual intelligence, which is the higher understanding of spiritual laws and the unity of all being, is reinforced by Ho'oponopono's four magic sentences. Features of this form of intelligence are level-headedness, a good capacity for the assessment of the self and our own powers (that we will absolutely not harm ourselves or others), as well as a good capacity for discriminating between what is beneficial and what hinders our development.

An old fable demonstrates how quickly we can harm ourselves and others if we do not possess, for example, a good capacity for discrimination:

A camel was drinking some water from a river when a scorpion spoke to him: 'Oh, dear camel, I must get very urgently to the other side of the river. My aunt is sick and is expecting me. Only I can help her in her need, because I know how to cook a good soup. Camels are known far and wide to be the best swimmers. Please be merciful and carry me across.' 'Hmm, you are a scorpion. I am afraid that if I let you climb on my back to take you across, you will sting me and then I must die,' answered the camel. To which the scorpion replied, 'Oh, how can you think I would do such a thing? If we are right in the middle of the river and I sting you, I will drown too. Trust me, I need you.' After these words, the camel knelt down and the scorpion clambered up onto one of its humps. The camel waded into the river. The two engaged in conversation and the scorpion had much to say about his family. When the camel and the scorpion had got to about the middle of the river, the scorpion let his sting sparkle in the sun and stung with all his might. His face distorted by pain, the camel asked, 'Why have you done that? Now we must both drown.' The scorpion replied, 'I could not do otherwise.'

We humans are not what we do once; we are what we do over and over again. We are our habits. Through the formal model of Ho'oponopono, we attain the necessary state of rest and relaxation to be able to say, 'No.'

A Ho'oponopono Exercise

In the following short but very powerful exercise we see Ho'oponopono's operation as an inner dialogue that creates a new program for our unconscious actions. It is a conversation with our subconscious, or as the Hawaiians say, a conversation with our inner child.

If you have recognised yourself in the story of the camel or know somebody who is glad to do things for others and yet remains unsatisfied because nobody fulfils their needs, it is a good opportunity for a Ho'oponopono. In this exercise we want forgiveness for having, in the past, cared insufficiently for ourselves and our own needs. We forgive ourselves and others for having uttered reproaches. Please lean back a moment and enter your heart. Then ask for forgiveness for having cared too little for your health. Say the four magic sentences, and repeat the exercise for all issues that come to mind.

I love you. Yes, I love you.
I am sorry. Please forgive me. Thank you.

Ho'oponopono in Practice

Ho'oponopono as Family Conference

The Hawaiian family is called 'ohana', meaning 'several plants with a common root', and as the saying goes, 'If one person in a family has a problem, they all have a problem.' Yes, that is understandable. Can we be happy and find peace in our hearts when anyone close to us is suffering? No, we are all bound together, one to another. Bound in our thoughts, bound in our hearts, in the morphogenetic field, and through our genes. Perhaps you have participated in a Family Constellation* and witnessed first-hand how very intensively we are all connected, even to people who are complete strangers.

Our workplace too is a sort of family. Many people spend more time there than at home and share more

---

* Developed in its modern form by German psychologist Bert Hellinger in the 1990s, Family Constellations is an experiential, therapeutic process that aims to release and resolve issues within and between people.

of their feelings there than with their relations. Does a colleague have a problem, is the boss in a bad mood or is someone being harassed? Then who has the problem? It's just the same at school – that too is a sort of family. If a student is insufficiently integrated into the community, he can, to gain some attention, hassle his fellow pupils or drive his teacher to the edge of insanity.

A traditional Ho'oponopono, such as a family conference, is divided into about 13 steps and in overview can be apportioned in four sections. The prerequisites for success are a common goal (which we wish to reach) and a common wish to grow. Fundamentally, the protection of children, of animals and plants, rivers and mountains takes first place. The Earth belongs to all and its preservation has foremost priority.

1. The Prayer (Pule)

In communal prayer, we each connect ourselves with Source, with God and the ancestors. Thereby, we raise ourselves to a higher level of energy. In other words: if we always do the same thing, e. g., because we have always done the same thing, we will always get the same result. In prayer, we recognise that we are directed to seek help, perhaps because we are stuck fast in a relationship pattern. However, instead of asking for the problem to be solved through another (Dear God, please make Ben have a thorough wash for once…), we ask for insight, intelligence, the strength to listen, and the courage to speak the truth. Then, finally, the conflict presents us with an opportunity for realisation and mutual growth.

2. Description of the Conflict (Mahiki)
In the second step of the process, one speaks about unfulfilled needs and expectations, but also about in-justice, rule infringements and pain.

3. Mutual Requests for and Guarantees of Forgiveness (Mihi and Kala)
In step three, all the participants look for their share of the problem. The well-trodden paths of the typical culprit-victim relationship are abandoned, and every-one is ready to search their hearts honestly for the

ways in which they themselves have contributed to the problem.

An Explanatory Example:

Someone in the family begins to drink. He neglects his duties, and further problems and conflicts arise in the family. There is an open question which everyone now asks in their hearts, 'If I have done something that has caused my brother to become dissatisfied with himself, and because of it start drinking, what was it?'

Perhaps earlier, someone has slighted him, argued with him, offended his girlfriend, not taken him seriously, etc., so that the brother has sought his solution in alcohol. 'What is my share in the cause of my brother's drinking?'

After everyone has spoken and cleansed their hearts, there follows a mutual and common request for and granting of forgiveness. The victim forgives the culprit, the culprit forgives the culprit, the culprit forgives the victim and the victim forgives the victim. Thereby the matter is 'oki', 'settled'.

4. Let Go *(Kala)* and the Common Prayer of Thanks *(Pule Hoʻopau)*

In step four, all speak together the prayer of thankfulness. Thankfulness is essential, for the matter is now with God, the angels and the ancestors, and they concern themselves with the transformation. It is our task to have trust in God's works and no longer act in the old, accustomed ways. Oki is very much oki. It is traditional to end a Hoʻoponopono with a communal meal.

We all live in various sorts of communal entities that we perceive as familial: the family itself, society, the town or the country. Humans belong to the mammalian family, and the name we give to the totality of our great family is the ecosystem. The field of application and the possibilities for Hoʻoponopono are very wide. Your colleagues are not perhaps ready to join with you to make a 'Hopopo – what?', but you can do it for them in spirit and watch what happens.

Before the sun goes down, forgive.

Hawaiian Proverb

Ho'oponopono as a Method of Personal Purification

Relationships and Partnerships

We are all spirits of God's Spirit (kane). We are God's children, and as brothers and sisters we have inherited a paradise. Our natural task is to maintain this paradise of Earth. Just as we have received the perfect gift of our bodies, so we live on Earth without needing to add anything to what has been given us. None of us has made the water, the air or the earth. Yet somehow, it is hard for us to live and work together.

As long as you live on your own, you can believe yourself to be a very sociable person. As a matter of fact, I always thought I was completely OK. However, not every one of my female partners shared this opinion. In a partnership or workplace, wherever people are close to one another, everyone very quickly notices a person's kinks. Everyone sees it, except the person in question.

Toothpaste comes out of a toothpaste tube when it is squeezed, and in the same way whatever is sticking inside a person emerges as soon as he meets a relationship challenge. Whether in a marriage or as a human being – one of our missions in life is learning to work together for the welfare of humanity, animals, plants and rocks.

A Hoʻoponopono Exercise

So, if you have difficulties with someone you should bless him or her and repeat again and again in spirit:

I am sorry. Please forgive me.
I love you. Thank you.

Remember this: every situation hides a learning opportunity. Make a list of every person, animal and plant with which you want to live in purity. Then, in your thinking, make a Hoʻoponopono with each one.

God sleeps in the rocks,
Dreams in the plants,
Awakens in the animals
And acts in the human beings.

Indian Proverb

Perhaps you live, or used to live, in an unhappy partnership, or you have just ended a relationship and still carry within you the hurts that must be healed. As long as we think of a relationship with resentment, hatred, sadness or disappointment, we will attract a similar relationship through the resonance principle, or generally block ourselves off from a new, harmonious and loving relationship. If you do not heal the wounds from old partnerships, it is very probable that the same wounds, renewed, will be inflicted on you again. Anger, hatred and bitterness are strong emotions that attract their targets with precision.

A Ho'oponopono Exercise

Please forgive yourself for having lived in a relationship that did you no good. The good that comes of it is that you now know better. You are thus a winner! Release yourself energetically from your old relationship, forgive your partner and free yourself. Forgive yourself unconditionally and say goodbye to all feelings of guilt.

Health

Jesus of Nazareth is counted as the greatest healer in the biblical history of the world. He healed the blind, the lame, the spiritually benighted and others too. But stop! In the biblical stories, he always emphasised that he did not heal the people, but their beliefs. We are healthy and healed in every moment when we recognise our perfection and complete the paradigm change. That can either happen spontaneously or it must be practiced, for example through affirmations, seeing ourselves as healthy and powerful, rather than needy and incomplete.

In a Hawaiian temple every physical healing is preceded by a Ho'oponopono, the reason being that the spirit must be healed before the body can be, for it is our consciousness that controls our material parts. We know from quantum physics that consciousness is the decisive factor in creating a reality out of the cloud of possibilities.

Another of world history's great doctors, Hippocrates, wrote on this same theme: 'There are no unhealable illnesses – only unhealable people.' To be healed means to be complete, because when we are sick, we lack something. But it is not health we lack, but belief and trust in our perfection. Perhaps we lack trust because we have not had the experience of perfection. A person who has never had an asthma attack experiences himself differently to someone who would like to get rid of their asthma under any circumstances.

'Gesundheit', the German word for health, contains the concept ,sund' which in Scandinavian refers to a ,strait' (a passage of water connecting two seas or other large bodies of water). ,Sund' is also contained in the English word ,sunder', meaning ,to split apart'.

The path to health can therefore be understood as overcoming the gulf that has divided us from our divine perfection, and Ho'oponopono shows us how to swim. While we are practicing the relinquishment of negative, destructive thoughts, words and deeds, we are re-entering into unity and divine harmony.

After Louise L. Hay, the author in the positive thinking realm, discovered the connection between spiritual and physical dispositions, she published the classic *Heal your Body* in 1976.* A few years later, her knowledge was put to the ultimate test – she got cancer. In an interview for her film *You Can Heal Your Life – The Movie*, she reported how her cancer had been healed by a thorough process of physical and spiritual detoxification. She was challenged by all the traumatic experiences of her childhood and she passed the test by releasing and forgiving everyone who had participated in them. In her therapeutic work she came to realise that her illness and the majority of her clients'

Louise L. Hay: *Heal Your Body A-Z. The Mental Causes for Physical Illness and the Way to Overcome Them.* Hay House, CA 1998.

illnesses and problems disappeared as soon as she and the clients began to accept themselves, forgive themselves and love themselves. 'I love you. I love myself.' 'I love you' means 'I love myself.' The subconscious makes no distinction between the inner and the outer.

If a person does not forgive himself for his past mistakes and believes he is guilty, he will become ill. In the end, he has to suffer and be punished for his mistakes. It is quite simple. If you continually scold yourself for something, you program your subconscious to destroy you. You will then either eat too much or too little, sleep too much or too little, perhaps work yourself to death or begin wanting to please everyone. If we punish and scold ourselves unconsciously, it can happen that our defective self-consciousness not only weakens our immune system but overdraws on our bank account. Then finally, anyone who is worthless has no money and deserves no reward.

Profession, Vocation and Compensation

Each of us possesses unique capabilities. These talents are our unique contribution to the wellbeing of the Whole. Each person bears within him a valuable treasure: his individual vocation. Vocation means that there is a calling within each of us, a purpose. When we follow this call, everything goes well. We are in tune with ourselves and with life. Our life now follows a plan that is bigger than we are.

Please imagine the following situation: you are lying on your deathbed, and your capabilities come in, and one after another they ask why you have not done more to develop them. Finally your dream enters, the dream that you have always had, and the dream asks, 'Why have you not lived me? I have spoken to you every day.' What will you say in reply?

A Ho'oponopono Exercise

If you still do not know your vocation, perhaps are unemployed or have a job that destroys you physically and spiritually, forgive yourself at once. Make a Ho'oponopono. Trust yourself and go through the four steps. Pass from the Shadow to the Light. Love and accept yourself unconditionally, whatever your present situation. Then vigorously direct all your attention to the solution.

Incoming letters tell of problems in the workplace, in finances, in partnership and with health. Especially in the workplace, we are confronted now and then by aggressive contemporaries. We might experience irrational decisions and must do things that run completely contrary to our own value systems.

Money is the expression of the value of our performance, our payment. A friend, for example, wants an atypically large honorarium for his work as a gardener. 'Because I love myself,' as he once said to me smiling, and he always does a good job – which is natural for people who love themselves and value their work. So, now begin to value yourself and raise your worth.

A person's bank balance is an expression, amongst others, of self-image, the image that we each have of ourselves. If the credit side of your bank account is constantly rising and falling, then you should ask yourself, quite simply, whether something parallel is happening within you. Search your heart for the reason, and then forgive yourself.

In a study performed in 2008 by Carnegie Mellon University called *Why Play A Losing Game?*, lead author Emily Haisley explored why people on low incomes play the lottery. The study found that in a short period of time after winning, the vast majority of American lottery millionaires were financially back where they were before they got their winnings, most even broke and in debt. Can it be that our reality is the direct result of our conditioning, thought pattern and type of relationship? Apparently, the cause lies in the spiritual and the effect in the material realms.

The Worldwide Political Challenge

If someone in the family has a problem, then everyone has a problem, and exactly the same pattern is true on the national, European and global planes. It is not only through the Internet that the world is being brought together, but also through modern modes of transport that allow us to reach every point of the Earth's surface in an ever shorter space of time. We see ourselves faced by great challenges: genocide, religious wars, energy crises, bank crises and corruption, unending streams of blood flowing from slaughterhouses, poverty and worldwide starvation, environmental catastrophes. Add, last but not least: for the last fifty years humankind has been producing something in such quantities that it threatens to choke us – rubbish.

What can an individual, what can you and I do? How can we emerge from the fog of apathetic powerlessness and self-sacrificing acquiescence – the attitude that says, 'In any case, there's nothing I can do?'

When you and I begin really to understand what faith and trust, words and feelings, the quantum laws, love and forgiveness can achieve, we possess a powerful tool to move world events in a positive direction.

Do you know about holograms? A hologram is an image with a special property. If you cut it to pieces and look at one of the new and very small pieces through a magnifying glass, you will always see the same image on each fragment. Stated metaphysically: as in the great, so in the small. A macrocosm in the microcosm. Our Universe is such a hologram. We live in a hologram.

You and I are parts of this Universe; we are parts and images of God. This means that the Universe and God also act through us. Take a step in the direction of 'making right right', and the whole Universe makes a leap towards harmony and peace. That bestows power and responsibility on every individual.

We can each begin with ourselves: if something disturbs you, if you would like to improve something or bring something on this planet into harmony, please put the following four questions to yourself:

1. Who has the problem?
2. Who is the problem?
3. Who has the power?
4. Who has the responsibility?

Please make a Ho'oponopono to all the questions and unconditionally forgive yourself and everyone who has in any way participated.

After you have moved yourself, and therefore the planet too, back from self-destruction to a place of love, make the paradigm change and look for new possibilities. Ask yourself this: if there were something I could do whereby I could be a part of the solution, what would it be? Simply direct your attention away from the problem and fix it on the solution.

We are all travelling
On a mutual journey.

Heal yourself,
And you heal the world,
Thank you.

Afterword

Aloha, dear Readers,

I hope that by reading my little book you have gained some valuable knowledge and are ready for your next personal steps. Perhaps you have become aware of things in your life that you want to alter or further develop. With my whole heart I wish you success in these endeavours.

You will find further information on the website www.hooponoponosecret.com. My especial thanks to the Hawaiian people for the tradition of Ho'oponopono and the great world service that is joined to it.

Mahalo nui loa, many thanks.
Me ke aloha pumehana, with heartfelt greetings,

Sincerely, Ulrich Duprée

Picture Credits

Marianne Mayer: page 7; Eva Browning: 8; William Wang: 14; mar
gouillat photo: 24; Natasha Art: 28; 808isgreat: 40; NorthShore Surf
Photos: 46; Ilja Mašik: 48; Marina Krasnovid: 51, 74; Melanie Diet-
erle: 52; NorthShoreSurfPhotos: 56; Katrina Brown: 58; Nadja: 64;
idreamphoto: 70; klikk: 80; Chad McDermott: 94; TAlex: Flower motif
next to Exercises. All fotolia.com

For further information and to request a book catalogue contact:
Inner Traditions, One Park Street, Rochester, Vermont 05767

Earthdancer Books is an Inner Traditions imprint.
Phone: +1-800-246-8648, customerservice@innertraditions.com
www.earthdancerbooks.com • www.innertraditions.com

EARTHDANCER

AN INNER TRADITIONS IMPRINT